Property of
BRIDGEPORT PUBLIC LIBRARY
Burroughs Building

S0-ADT-995

PENGUIN BOOKS

MARCEL MARCEAU: MASTER OF MIME

Ben Martin is a photographer, journalist, and documentary filmmaker who has been associated for many years with *Time-Life*. A man of wide travel and wide interests, he has had his work published in most of the world's major magazines. He is a pilot and trained scuba diver, has visited most parts of the globe, has studied Chinese and Japanese, and has met and worked with many celebrities, from John F. Kennedy and Aleksei Kosygin to Marcel Marceau. Ben Martin's photographs also contributed to the success of Christopher Matthew's *A Different World: Stories of Great Hotels*.

DATE DUE

OCT 17 2000

Marcel Marceau

MASTER OF MIME

Ben Martin

PENGUIN BOOKS

Property of
BRIDGEPORT PUBLIC LIBRARY
Burroughs Building

A779.20924
M313m
1979 ed.
(1)

Penguin Books Ltd, Harmondsworth,
Middlesex, England
Penguin Books, 625 Madison Avenue,
New York, New York 10022, U.S.A.
Penguin Books Australia Ltd, Ringwood,
Victoria, Australia
Penguin Books Canada Limited, 2801 John Street,
Markham, Ontario, Canada L3R 1B4
Penguin Books (N.Z.) Ltd, 182–190 Wairau Road,
Auckland 10, New Zealand

First published in Great Britain by Paddington Press Ltd 1978
First published in the United States of America by
Paddington Press Ltd 1978
Published in Penguin Books 1979

Copyright © Paddington Press (U.K.) Limited, 1978
All rights reserved

LIBRARY OF CONGRESS CATALOGING IN PUBLICATION DATA
Martin, Ben, 1930–
    Marcel Marceau, master of mime.
    1. Marceau, Marcel—Portraits, etc.   2. Mimes—France—Portraits.   I. Title.
[PN1986.M3M33 1979]   779'.2'0924   79-15449
ISBN 0 14 00.5362 X

Printed in the United States of America by
Rae Publishing Co., Inc., Cedar Grove, New Jersey
Set in Photo Garamond

Except in the United States of America,
this book is sold subject to the condition
that it shall not, by way of trade or otherwise,
be lent, re-sold, hired out, or otherwise circulated
without the publisher's prior consent in any form of
binding or cover other than that in which it is
published and without a similar condition
including this condition being imposed
on the subsequent purchaser

Contents

For Kathryn with love.

Preface

HAVE BEEN AN unashamed fan of Marcel Marceau since I first saw him in New York in the early 1960s. No, it wasn't in the theater—it was in an elevator of the Essex House Hotel on New York's Central Park South. I had been photographing the chairman of an electronics company for the business pages of *Time* magazine, and was waiting to descend with the executives' public relations man. As the elevator doors opened I was instantly fascinated by the only occupant. Not only did he have a face of great character (I immediately felt he would be a good camera subject) but the very attitude of his body struck an amusing chord. He seemed to be leaning against an invisible mantelpiece or door frame, although this very well-dressed and obviously continental gentleman was standing quite normally—or was he?

One night more recently, in my home in London, I saw this look again—without makeup, without costume. He seemed to be leaning against the mantelpiece, though he was at least five feet from the fireplace. Marceau was being Bip without knowing it. It is just the way he is. And I hope that is the way I have presented him here. This book is not meant to be an all-encompassing biography of a great theatrical figure but rather one photojournalist's view of the man as a performer and friend. Though it does begin at the beginning, I'll leave the details to Marceau himself, for someday he will write his autobiography, and I for one can hardly wait for it to roll off the presses.

As we left that elevator the P.R. man whispered to me: "That was Marcel Marceau." I had never seen him perform, but I made a point to buy a ticket and see his show at the City Center. I've been a fan ever since.

I was not introduced to Marceau for several more years. He was appearing in London, and a friend of mine from Paris, Robert Pledge, had arranged for Marceau to write the introduction to a portfolio of dance photographs. He was in London to go over the article with Marceau and invited me to see the show, and later he introduced me to him. Several days later Marceau called and asked me to make an informal photograph of him without makeup or costume for use in the program of his next French tour. Working with the man for only a short time so stimulated me that I knew I had to do more than just one photograph.

Marceau was preparing his new show, *The Creation of the World*, and I convinced *Life* magazine that there was a story worth doing—and only *Life* with its style of photography and way of working was the place for it. Though a bit skeptical, they agreed to back the project, and I began the task of recording Marceau creating *The Creation of the World*.

It was his first venture into producing audiovisual and cinematic effects to accompany his mime program, and it was an arduous task for both of us. For him there were seemingly insurmountable technical problems making the lights, slide and cinema projectors, tape decks, and everything else go together properly. For this was his creation and although he had at times a crew of twenty or thirty technicians working on a problem it was his show. Marceau is like that. He throws his all into something until it is done—and done brilliantly—and he is on the point of exhaustion.

For several weeks there were sixteen- and eighteen-hour days at the Théâtre des Champs Élysées on Avenue Montaigne in Paris. There were days when slide projectors would not synchronize with music or maddeningly chewed up valuable slides. There were days when I shot twenty rolls of film—and days spent exhaustingly to shoot five frames. There were weekends at the farmhouse in Berchère, communal dinners with all of the technicians and crew—where talk of work was supposed to be taboo and where the conversation always drifted back to the problems at hand.

Finally came the opening: the grueling weeks of preparation paid off, and after the run in Paris there were plans for a tour of the United States, where we felt the technical innovations of an audiovisual presentation would be enthusiastically received. I was to accompany Marceau to provide the American view for *Life*.

But then came the blow—*Life* magazine closed. No more would there be unlimited film and dedicated technicians in Paris and New York to process it and to make prints that captured every nuance of the subject's performance. No more the dream of giant pages that showed a photographer's work better than any other medium in the world.

One night after a subdued dinner at the farmhouse in Berchère I showed Marceau the fruits of those months of work. He jumped up. "But you have enough photographs for a book," he said. So was reborn the idea— and now after several more years of photographing Marceau in Europe, England and America it has come to fruition—a camera portrait of Marcel Marceau, Master of Mime.

BEN MARTIN
London 1978

A Brief History of Mime

MIMICRY IS A basic form of language. Most of us have probably gone through the experience in a foreign country, when not speaking the language, of making the motions of eating or drinking to get across our thoughts or needs to a local inhabitant. In doing so we become mimes.

Therefore it seems likely that a form of mime was the earliest language. The primitive caveman gesturing and acting out his feelings to his companions had no other way to communicate. He dramatized his prowess as a hunter or warrior, accompanying his motions with grunts and snarls until a spoken language finally evolved. Today primitive tribes still act out entire stories in their dances, and through this form of mimicry their mythology and the history of their ancestors live on.

Mime as a true theatrical form began in ancient Greece, where performers portrayed the events of everyday life with the help of elaborate gestures. Mime was not the silent show we recognize today. Before each performance in the Athenian theater the actors often did a mime show as an introduction. The principal mimes were called *ethologues*, meaning painters of manners, and they tried to teach moral lessons in their work. During the performances themselves the choruses mimed as they spoke and reacted in movement to what occurred on the stage.

Then there were the popular entertainers of all kinds—jugglers, acrobats, musicians, male and female alike—who thronged the festivals and market places, or who might be hired to perform in private homes. Some might have a special gift for mimicry, who could imitate the sound of thunder or the cries of animals and birds. Their ability to use every limb and every muscle, and to control their facial expressions, set them apart from other performers. A rough platform might raise the actors above the heads of the crowd, and a colleague would collect coins from the spectators. Language was no barrier to this art of noise, movement and facial expression, and the simple requirements of a platform and curtain could be improvised everywhere. The gulf was wide, however, between these performers and the actors who, in mask and costume, appeared at the Festival of Dionysus to present the tragedies of Euripides or the comedies of Menander.

As literature, the mime developed through the writings of such dramatists as Sophron (in the fifth century B.C.) and later (in the second century B.C.), Herondas, fragments of whose work have survived to this day. They are realistic and sometimes sordid studies of certain social types and were probably intended to be read rather than acted.

At its highest point the most elaborate form of mime, known as the *hypothesis* and performed by a company, may have approached the level of true drama. It differed, however, in its preoccupation with the establishment and development of character rather than of plot, and there is record of solo performers who prided themselves on their ability to give the impression that they were several individuals.

The contacts of Roman with Greek during the third century B.C., at the time of Pyrrhus' campaigns in southern Italy, probably made many Romans familiar with mime at a time when the literary drama of Rome had hardly begun. The Festival of Flora was initiated a few years after the introduction of Greek drama to the Roman stage, and like the Greek Festival of Dionysus it became a favorite occasion for the performers of mimes. The festival was celebrated riotously by the population, and it went so far as to allow the appearance of mime actresses naked on the stage.

An element of indecency clung to the mime from the beginning, and it reached an incredible level during the Roman empire. Emperor Heliogabalus is said to have ordered the performance of sex acts on stage, and if the plot included an execution sometimes a condemned criminal would be substituted for the actor to give the spectators an extra thrill.

As Christianity asserted itself opposition grew to the bawdy traditions and associations of mime, and in turn the Church received the scornful attentions of the actors during their performances—until the Church got the upper hand, excommunicating all performers and later closing down all the theaters. Yet basic mime survived. Its requirements were so simple that it could still be performed anywhere, in public or in private. Eventually from the tenth century on, the Church relaxed its attitude, began to accept the theater, and indeed rather than condemning it began to patronize it. Mystery and morality plays began to appear with religious themes, many performed in mime.

So mime continued to entertain the masses throughout the Middle Ages and on to modern times. It passed through varying degrees of popularity, reaching its height in sixteenth-century Italy, in the form of *Commedia dell' Arte*. In 1576 a company of Italian players led by Flamino Scala went to France, where the art of mime, and of *Commedia dell' Arte* in particular, became immensely popular. Many of the traditional gestures and figures, such as Harlequin, became familiar at this time.

It was almost two and a half centuries later, in 1811, when a Bohemian acrobatic family touring the continent played at the Parisian Fairs. The son, Jean Gaspard Deburau, was engaged to play at the Funambules on the Boulevard du Temple, a home of tumblers and tightrope walkers. He remained at this theater until his death, and during this time changed mime from crude slapstick to the art form it is considered today. Deburau created with great subtlety his characterization of the pale, lovesick Pierrot, the eternal seeker, and left us the legacy that today is echoed in Marcel Marceau's own creation, Bip. After Deburau's death his son Charles carried on in his father's tradition. Though of lesser stature, his influence was powerful both in Marseilles, where he taught Rouffe and his son Severin, and in Paris, where one-act mimes were being performed at the Opéra.

Mime received new impetus after the First World War from the great Jacques Copeau, who taught Charles Dullin at the Vieux-Colombier school. Étienne Decroux, who had been another pupil, took these beginnings a stage further, and together with his own pupil Jean-Louis Barrault developed the first elements of modern mime. Barrault later went his own way, to create the first true mimodramas.

Then after the Second World War emerged Marceau, a pupil of Decroux at the Dullin school. Heir to a tradition over two thousand years old, he took mime as it was then known, studied, honed, improved and transformed it. He was the architect of a totally new style and tradition, the true creator and master of modern mime as we understand it today.

"Mime is not a silent art.
It is the art of touching people."

MARCEAU AND I were sitting in the garden of his home in the countryside outside Paris. It was a beautiful spring day and he had just finished making new plans with his gardener. We were talking about his future projects and he expanded on a feeling which has increasingly disturbed him. "I am a prisoner of my art. People do not want to see me speak, or use props or appear as a character other than Bip or the stylized mime that I have created. They are uneasy with a Marceau that is unfamiliar."

Uneasy his public may be, but there is far more to Marcel Marceau than just the mime character we see on stage. Husband, father, artist, writer, linguist, collector—he is all these things and more.

He was born on March 22, 1923, the younger son of a butcher named Mangel, in Strasbourg, France—the capital of Alsace-Lorraine and practically astride the French–German border.

Influenced by his Jewish upbringing and his father's socialism, Marcel grew up with idealistic political views. Even today he asks, "Must the artist be the fool of society? Does he exist just to make us smile? No—he must be political."

And though his is not a partisan stance, there's no denying that Marceau is political. His works cry out for understanding, for help between people. He is like us all—and that is why he is so popular around the world.

In school, young Marcel was quiet and shy, by his own admission even docile. Every piece of schoolwork was done perfectly, and there was always the need to perform. After school, when he was only seven, the neighborhood children would crowd round outside his house begging him to come and make them laugh.

By the time he was nine he was the star attraction at his aunt's summer day camp, and many parents would only send their children back the next year if Marcel was there to entertain them. This love of performing—of being center-stage—developed early, and Marcel's thoughts began to turn to a professional theatrical career.

The year 1939 brought war, and the Mangels were among the first of millions of people to be uprooted. The first day of France's entry into World War II, the people of Strasbourg were given two hours to pack no more than sixty pounds of personal belongings each, and those who wished were shipped by truck and train to southwest France.

Marcel and his brother Alain were among those who fled. Within a short time, Alain, barely out of his teens, was a leader of the underground in Limoges and his younger brother Marcel became one of the liaison men.

Part of Marcel's job was easy for a young man of artistic talents. With red wax crayons and drawing ink he changed the ages on the identity cards of scores of French youths, making them too young to be sent to labor camps.

But another part of his job was not so easy and he doesn't like to talk about that very much. His task was to lead across the border children whose parents were in the Underground or wanted by the Nazis. Disguised as boy scouts and campers, they went high into the Alps, out of occupied France and into the safety of Switzerland. There were many trips up into the mountains, and hundreds of children were saved, and he wonders, "Would I have the courage to do it again?"

In 1944 his father was captured and sent to Auschwitz. His name was not even registered before he was taken to the crematorium. His mother survived, and Marceau visits her often at her home in the south of France.

About the same time Alain's picture appeared on the wanted list on the wall of Gestapo headquarters. Limoges became too dangerous for Marcel and he was sent to Paris where he registered under the name Marcel Marceau. Marcel Mangel had ceased to exist two years earlier when Alain had arranged for a false identity card for his younger brother. Ironically, the surname he chose was that of a general of the French Revolution.

At school in Limoges he had studied decorative art, specializing in enamel work, but in Paris he turned more and more to theater and became a student of Charles Dullin at his school of dramatic art.

When he entered theater school Marceau wanted to be an actor. He had always been fascinated by the films of Keaton and Chaplin and he says, "To me Chaplin was an actor." It was only later that he learned about mime and became a student of Étienne Decroux before being called up to serve in the First French Army, the army of occupation.

After being demobilized and while still a student he joined the theatrical company of Jean-Louis Barrault, another of Decroux's former students.

When he turned to mime the other students laughed. He says, "We were alone on stage, making funny movements and not speaking." They would ask, "How can you survive two hours on a stage without words?" But survive he did, and soon he attracted acclaim for his role of Arlequin in *Baptiste*, at the Théâtre de Marigny.

Baptiste was adapted from a French film, *Les Enfants du Paradis* (*The Children of Paradise*), which was a fictional biography of the great Deburau. In the film Barrault played Deburau and Decroux played Deburau's father.

Marcel based much of his mime on Harlequin and the character of Deburau's Pierrot, and by 1947 had evolved from this his own character Bip, which he first played at the tiny Théâtre de Poche (Pocket Theater) in Paris. "Decroux had first introduced me to the role of Arlequin," he says, "and when I did my research I kept wondering why such a character couldn't become part of the twentieth century." This lovable white-faced clown with bell-bottomed trousers, striped sailor's pullover and a beflowered opera hat also owes much to Chaplin's pathetic bowlered waif. Chaplin and Keaton are still Marceau's idols, as I recently witnessed in Los Angeles' Disneyland. After a VIP tour of the most prominent attractions with his wife Anne, Marceau was asked by the guide if there was anything else he would like to see. Without hesitation he said, "Yes, the old silent movie theater," and we watched fascinated as he stood for an hour devouring with his eyes the scratchy faded silent films.

In the same year as Bip's creation Marceau made his first tour, which included Switzerland, Italy, Belgium and Holland. His audience was growing.

The following year Marcel Marceau received the Deburau Prize for his mimodrama, *Death Before Dawn*, and over the next twelve years wrote and directed more than twenty-five more mimodramas. But he was still known mainly by an intellectual minority until his first U.S. tour in 1955.

The first run of two weeks at New York's Phoenix Theater had to be extended, moving to another Broadway theater, the Ethel Barrymore, and finally to the larger City Center. The total run was six months. "After that, big cities and universities all welcomed me, but it was Red Skelton's TV Special that really opened up a mass audience I otherwise would never have reached." He broadened that audience by appearing on television with other stars such as Fred Astaire, Victor Borge, Mike Douglas and Dinah Shore, and he credits the children who saw him on the Skelton show with pulling in their parents to see "Marcel."

The TV variety shows brought Marceau's talents as a mime to the mass audience and won him two Emmy Awards. But it was the talk shows of Dick Cavett, Johnny Carson, Merv Griffin and David Frost that showed this audience the articulate side of this talented artist.

Marcel speaks fluent French, English, German, Spanish and Italian and more than just a smattering of several other languages, but he needs none of them to gain the appreciation of his audiences around the world. In 1966 Marceau and his company were flown to New York from Paris solely to present entertainment for the annual dinner of the "Presidents Club" at the Waldorf Astoria Hotel. The membership of this exclusive organization is made up of the chief executives of some of the world's mightiest corporations. Guests of honor that night were the President of the United States, Lyndon Johnson, and his family.

The following year Marceau received a letter from the director of Berlin's Tegel Penitentiary, who had heard that the mime had performed at prisons in Paris. He asked if he would do the same in Germany. Without hesitation Marceau accepted, and the prisoners cheered his performance at length. He has since often appeared at prisons in Europe and the United States.

In May 1970 Marceau performed in Hanoi, the capital of North Vietnam, and found the city placid: "I had the feeling there was no war going on, so kind were the people and so warm the welcome."

Six months later he was in New York performing, and took the time to break his silence and read excerpts from *War and Peace* on radio in company with other well-known artists, performers and business leaders.

Then in 1973 Marcel Marceau was awarded an honorary degree— L.H.D., Pantomimist—by Linfield College in the United States.

Marceau has appeared in six feature films and more than twenty shorts and television films, and has written and illustrated numerous books, including one for children, entitled *The Story of Bip*, containing his fanciful paintings of Bip soaring around the world.

He is an accomplished artist and his paintings have been exhibited in some of the world's leading galleries. Many of his works are in a primitive folk style not unlike that of the Haitian school or of Grandma Moses. Others take the broad, decisive ink and brush strokes of the Japanese calligrapher. He loves painting but laments the lack of time to practice it, so he ends up painting late at night. "Painting is my hobby," says Marceau, "but if I were not a mime it would be my art. Then I could devote the time to it that it needs. A true artist should show only the very best of his work, and I would need more than one lifetime if I were to paint as I would like to do, and continue being a mime." His paintings have sold very well, and art critics respect him as a painter and not merely as the novelty of a mime who happens to paint.

Over the years critics have recognized Marceau's genius and have almost always been unanimous in their praise for his abilities. In his turn, Marceau is generally kind to them:

> Critics are sometimes right and sometimes wrong—but the great critics are not those who say good things about you, but are those who know about theater. In time you sense it. Everybody makes mistakes. As an artist can do good work and bad work, so critics can sometimes be wrong too.
>
> Never has a critic prevented a great artist from developing, and those artists who truly have something to say are able to gain their fame with the help of critics—or in spite of them.

One of the best known of today's critics, Clive Barnes of the *New York Times*, touched a familiar chord when he said almost poetically in a review praising Marceau's performance, "How we love the invisible mantel shelves he so casually leans against." Marceau has many scrapbooks overflowing with reviews and interviews, but newspaper clippings are the least of his collections. His home is like a museum, with the clutter of wondrous things he has brought back from his travels around the world: icons, Russian boxes, pre-Columbian sculpture, Mexican pottery, Japanese dolls, lead soldiers, toys from every nation he has visited—and masks, especially Noh masks from Japan. They fill every shelf, every corner of every room. But the Noh masks are much more than just a collection, they are symbolic of the respect Marceau has for the arts of the East, and of his fascination with the human face.

> Kabuki and Noh are the forms of oriental art that appeal the most to me because they are very dramatic and very mimetic. The actors' faces are painted white or they use masks and they use stylized gestures. In a funny way, we have influenced them too. When I played in Japan my style character or my character Bip brought something different to them, it gave them something Greek, something Roman—something Marceau.

Catching the butterfly is different the way they do it. The Chinese have a symbolic catching of the butterfly, but not in the same way I do. I brought them something new.

The Mask Maker was certainly influenced by Japanese drama, but they have nothing like it. A former member of my troupe, Alexander Godorowski, suggested it to me in 1959. He said, "You should do a story of a man who puts on many faces. He has a funny mask that he cannot remove—and then the tragedy begins." It is now one of my best-received pieces. Through an idea a mime can create, but he must have a knowledge of style to be able to do it.

Music is another influence on Marceau's life and his art. He uses it effectively as a background for almost all of his repertory, and the range is extraordinary—from Bach, Vivaldi and Mozart through Ravel to Pink Floyd. Marceau believes Mozart to be the greatest mime musician ever and claims that Mozart inspired his most ambitious piece, *The Creation of the World*, with his Concerto no. 21 for Piano and Orchestra.

And in another way Marcel Marceau has tried to create his own world in a quiet village in the French countryside. It is a world of calm and beauty; a bronze Bip peers from behind a tree and flowers and fruit abound. Dogs and children play and a pair of ponies grazes contentedly.

Married three times, Marceau has two grown sons, Baptiste and Michel, and two young daughters, Camille and Aurelia. His wife Anne, who is a writer, has collaborated in the creation of some of his pantomimes, among them *The Tree* and *The Falcon*. Marcel and Anne and the two little girls live in a 250-year-old farmhouse in the village of Berchère sous Vègres, just an hour's drive from Paris. Next door Marceau has constructed an *atelier* in the same style as his home, and it is here that he paints and writes and perfects his pantomimes before a practice mirror. And it is here that he relaxes after the grueling tours that leave him near to exhaustion. He often speaks of his home, and to hear him talk of his feelings for Berchère and the work he has done there gives additional insight into the complexities of the man:

When I first bought the old farmhouse there were only four trees on the whole property. Now there are over 3,000 trees and bushes. In fifteen or twenty years I have created a real forest. It's not pride or vanity. To me trees are the symbols of life. We must be like trees. Man is still too selfish. We have the feeling that when we die we are finished. That is not so. As trees and flowers are renewed by other trees and flowers, so man must be renewed by man. We must live through others and others will live through us.

An appropriate thought, for Marceau has recently been given a grant by the French government to reopen his International School of Mime in Paris, and to form a company of pantomime artists from around the world.

In 1949, following his winning of the Deburau Prize, Marceau formed the Compagnie de Mime Marcel Marceau, the only company of pantomimists in the world at that time. Now, thanks to Marceau's popularity and influence, there are many schools and troupes of mime in countries as varied as Poland, Sweden, Russia, the United States, Switzerland and Britain. Touring and his increasing popularity as a solo performer, as well as the lack of subsidy, finally forced Marceau to disband the successful company in 1960 and leave his friend Pierre Verry in Paris to head the school.

Verry, like Marceau, had studied with Decroux and had joined Marceau's company in 1951 at the Studio des Champs Élysées. He appeared in major roles in each of the mimodramas, beginning with Marceau's adaptation of Gogol's *The Overcoat*, and has continued his association with Marceau as the Presenter of Cards on nearly every tour. His fanciful costumes and interpretative stances continue to delight audiences everywhere he appears with Marceau.

Marceau got to know Chaplin and many other great silent film stars, and he says of them, "Ironically, except for Chaplin and Harpo Marx, they were all considered passé by the time I met them, and their wealth had disappeared, but the fascinating thing about them, Sennett and Stan Laurel in particular, was that their poverty did not make them bitter. I think that is part of their genius. Money was not what their lives were about." Marceau tells of having tea, silver service and all, with Stan Laurel and his wife, who despite their poverty insisted upon observing all the formalities. He says, "Stan was immensely generous in advising me and pushing me beyond my natural boundaries."

But while acknowledging his debt to the old film stars he admires so much, Marceau is conscious of the gulf between their style of mime and his. He continued to elaborate on this difference, and from his remarks we can grasp the importance both of the tradition from which he has emerged and of the original genius which has enabled him to transcend it:

My art is an elusive art. It is making the abstract concrete and the concrete abstract. That is, making the invisible visible and the visible invisible. Whereas the silent film makers were surrounded by props, scenery and real people, in my one-man show I could not be surrounded by stylized props and physical people: it is the art of illusion by itself.

If Chaplin and Keaton had been mimes of the theater they would probably have played in the same way that I do. In their time they would have had a technique of their own which would have been a mixture of ballet, acrobatics and theatrical psychological acting. In the beginning I was related to them psychologically and physically, but the more I went into my work the more I had to take distance and create my own work and style.

I'm not a traditional mime at all. I have created something totally new out of necessity. We do not know exactly how the ancient mimes played. Precise instructions were never written down, so it has been up to each new generation of mimes to create their own style. Musicians are lucky—they have it all written down from the early times. Now, however, we can leave through films and videotape examples of our contemporary styles for future mimes to study.

In developing my style I had to proceed in two ways. I established two parts to my show—one, *pantomime du style*, to show the audience all of the possibilities of mime movements, such as walking against the wind, going up and down stairs, the tug of war. These were all the rudiments that one learns from a master such as Decroux—those things are passed on from one generation to another. But then I created new dramas with satire such as *The Trial*, *The Cage*, *The Creation of the World*. These have evolved into a whole new catalog of movements that have nothing more to do with Chaplin and Keaton.

It is interesting to wonder—if they had not been in the movies, if they had developed their art in the theater instead of on the screen—just how far they could have gone with new developments in their art.

The second part of my show was the character Bip, who was not the immortal figure or a symbol of a tree, a stone, a fish. Bip is a mortal man who can sometimes win but is most often beaten down. He is at the bottom of the ladder. It is here that I am most like Chaplin. Bip feels. And everyone knows how he feels. This then is my art.

In Close-up

THOUGH HE HAS appeared in films and on television, the medium through which Marceau is best known, and in which he feels most at home, is that of the theater or concert hall: his "art of touching people" finds its best expression through the powerful immediacy of the live stage performance. And yet the movement, the lighting, the distance are virtues which can sometimes work to the artist's disadvantage if every gesture, every nuance, cannot readily be seen and understood.

I suggested a studio session in which to take posed close-up shots to overcome this problem. Marceau had grave misgivings. Not only was he very busy (I had only just managed to extract from him a promise to give me some of his time during a very hectic tour of the United States) but he was afraid that to perform in an empty room would result in empty photographs—clumsy, artificial and lifeless. Once persuaded, however, he couldn't be restrained—and he gave me as much during the ensuing performance, despite my constant pauses to check equipment, adjust lights or change film, as he would before any of the capacity crowds he encounters around the world.

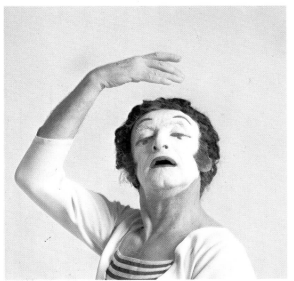

On Stage

No LINES TO learn, a simple costume, few props and no set: it all
looks so easy. But this is the greatest illusion of them all. Marceau works
with staggering dedication not only at his performance but at the technical
preparations. Lights, projectors, music—all must be perfect before the
makeup goes on and Verry, Marceau's friend of many years and his Presenter
of Cards, walks on stage.

Here we see Marceau directing his technicians, rehearsing, making up,
performing. Earlier bustle is forgotten as a huge auditorium is entranced by
the pale-faced figure under the spotlight. This is art, this has made those long
hours of planning, discussion and sheer physical effort worthwhile, and the
audience loves it.

And backstage he receives more personal applause and congratulation
from colleagues and friends. This is a time to relax, perhaps, and bathe in the
enthusiasm and appreciation of those around him. But Marceau is
wondering, "Was it good? How can we improve it? Perhaps for the next
show we ought to . . . ."

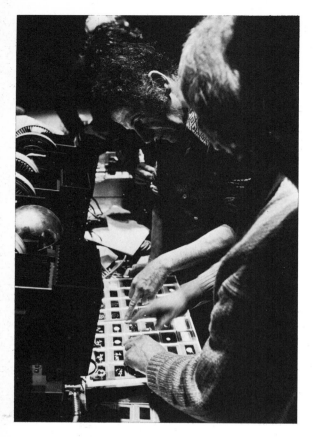

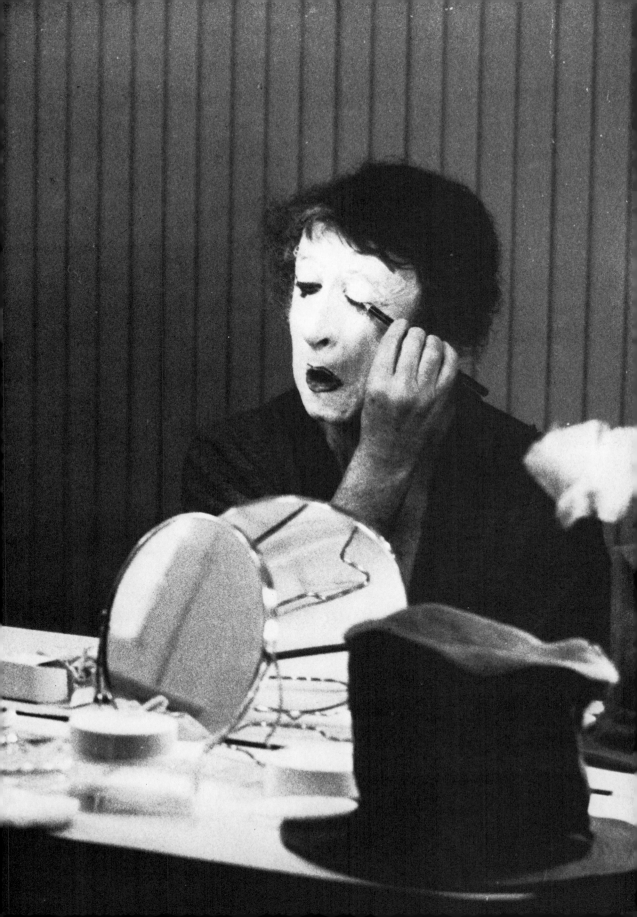

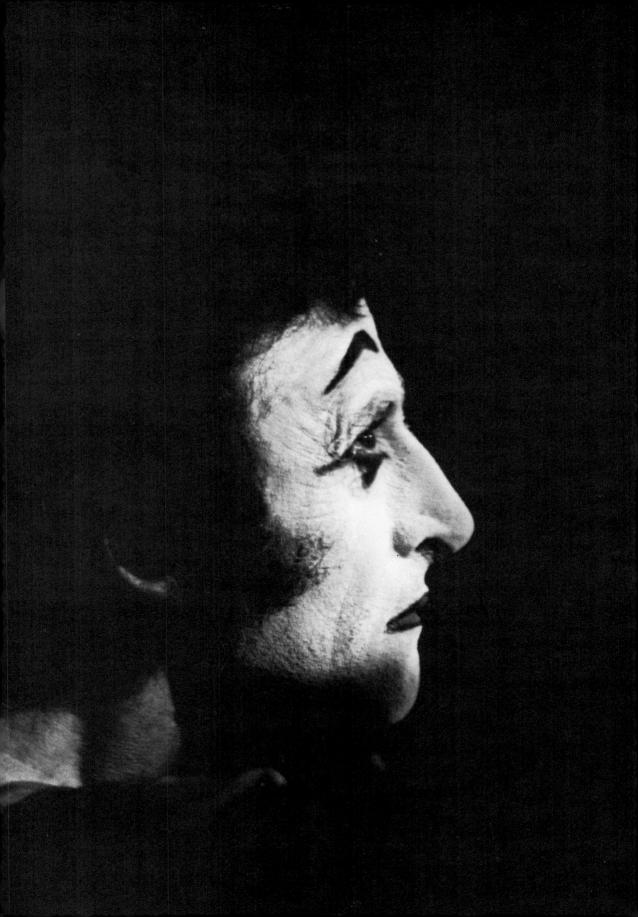

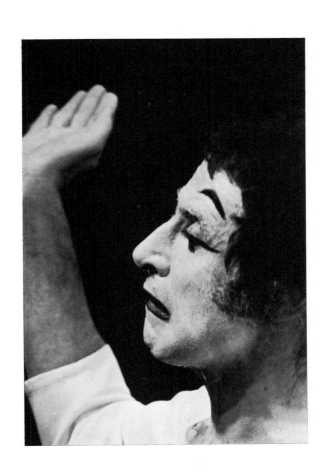

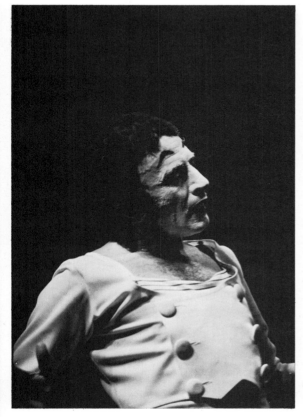

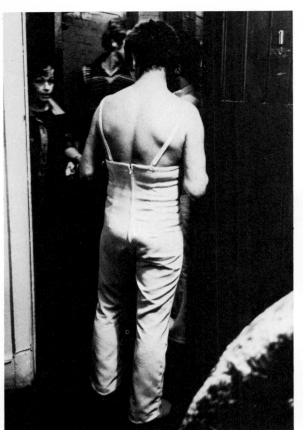

Off Stage

HERE AT BERCHÈRE in the French countryside there is tranquillity. With his wife Anne and their children, Marceau relaxes. But relaxation does not mean inactivity—indeed, even without the greasepaint the real Marceau is still difficult to pin down, so diverse are his pursuits and interests.

During the brief periods of freedom there is time to ride, paint, or tend to his lush, beautiful gardens. Among his collections of dolls, toys and masks he can play with the children or entertain friends. But the work is never far away: he has a practice room fitted with barre and mirrors where he exercises.

Sometimes, however, opportunities to relax occur in the middle of work. On his last American tour a visit to Los Angeles culminated in a trip to Disneyland, and in his own Paris there was time for some fun by the Eiffel Tower.

These interludes are all too infrequent. As he says himself, he is a prisoner of his art, and his thoughts and activities inevitably return to mime. But perhaps an excessively full life is the price one must pay, and the reward one must receive, for so enriching the lives of others.

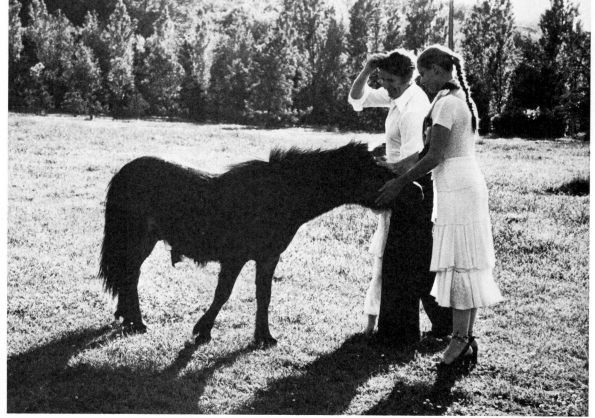

Technical Information

FOR THOSE photographers, amateur or professional, who might be interested in how these photographs were taken, I include this short section of technical information.

The project was undertaken with a variety of cameras and lenses, which were chosen to suit various situations. Motorized cameras, although ideal for sequences such as those Marceau performs, were generally found to be too noisy for use in the theater.

However, for the first section, "In Close-up," the black-and-white photographs were taken in natural daylight using a motorized Nikon with the 105mm $f2.5$ Nikkor lens. For most of the color photographs in the same section the Hasselblad camera was used with a specially designed electronic flash unit, although natural daylight was used in some. Three flash heads firing 800 watt-seconds of light from an Ascor powerpack were directed into a 25-square-foot diffusion box, giving the soft, nearly shadowless light. The Hasselblad 50, 85, 150 and 250mm lenses were used with an eye-level prism finder.

For the other sections of the book, Leica M-2 and M-4 cameras with 21, 35 and 50mm Leitz lenses and a 25mm Canon lens were used where quiet and unobtrusive work was required. The 35 and 50mm lenses were almost always used at or near their maximum aperture of $f1.4$. For the rest of the photography Nikon and Nikkormat cameras were used with lenses of 16, 20,

24, 55, 105, 180, 500 and 1000mm focal lengths. The Nikkor 43–86mm and Vivitar 85–205mm zoom lenses were also utilized. For the extreme close-up shots of Marceau's face in the performance sequence, the Nikkor 1000mm mirror lens was coupled with a 2x tele-extender to give an effective focal length of 2000mm and an extremely small aperture of $f22$. An extension tube to enable close focusing was also attached, and the complete combination was used on a unipod, allowing a shutter speed of 1/60 second under the bright stage lighting of Paris's Théâtre des Champs Élysées. Camera position was backstage in the wings, 30 to 50 feet from Marceau on center stage. Film speed was increased one to two stops.

The black-and-white film used was Kodak Tri-X, rated normally at ASA 400 in most circumstances. However, low light levels occasionally necessitated pushing the speed to 800 or 1600 ASA. Kodak D-76 developer was used in all cases.

Kodachrome and Ektachrome were the choice for color film and were used at their normal film speed ratings, except for High Speed Ektachrome Daylight and Tungsten, which were sometimes pushed one or two stops in extremely low light situations. Polacolor Professional Type 668 was used in a Hasselblad adapter for studio tests.

Acknowledgments

I would like to thank Dick Stolley, *People* magazine, New York; Jacques André and Louis Molinier, formerly of the *Life* photo lab, Paris; Gordon Bishop, London; John Alexander Colour Laboratory, London; CKP Colour Laboratory, London; Dan Esgro and Malcolm Lubliner Studio, Graphicolor Laboratory and Julian Wasser, all of Los Angeles; and the managements of the Théâtre des Champs Élysées, Paris, the John F. Kennedy Center, Washington, and the many other theaters throughout Europe and the United States for their kind cooperation.

My very special thanks to Graham Wiremu, Richard Johnson and John and Janet Marqusee of Paddington Press for their enthusiasm, direction and assistance.

Of course, without the cooperation of Marcel Marceau, his family and staff, this book would not have been possible: to them my heartfelt appreciation.